Expand Your Brand

Personal Branding for
Independent Consultants

TANYA STEVENSON

Copyright © 2018 by Tanya Stevenson

All rights reserved. This book or any portion thereof may not be reproduced, stored in a retrieval system, used in any manner whatsoever, or transmitted in any form or by any means-electronic, mechanical, digital, photocopy, recording, or any other without the express written permission of the publisher except for the use of brief quotations in printed book reviews.

WHAT YOU CAN TAKE AWAY FROM THIS BOOK

This book is my process for building a personal brand. I share the steps I took to get from being an unknown commodity to being a known value providing authority. These principles changed my career, my business, and the lives of the clients and consultants I've worked with—they are also what have allowed me to build a successful coaching program.

Most of you don't know me, but my story is somewhat unusual

I spent some of my childhood in the foster system. It was difficult, but it also made me who I am. At a young age, I vowed I would build a better life for myself, so I went from being the first person in my family to go to university to becoming a department leader and internal consultant to running my own consulting and coaching firm (throughout several recessions)—all without an MBA.

I have often attributed my results to being willing to do the hard work and being tenacious enough to go after what I wanted. However, as time passed, I realised that my focused, brute force wasn't the only factor—the fact that I discovered **personal branding** early in my career has defined much of my success. It's how I have been able to communicate *who I am* to the world, and the world has chosen to respond.

Apply these steps to go where you really want to go in your career and business

When I coach one-on-one with clients or teach classes, my ultimate goal is to figure out what my clients or students *really want to achieve*. I try to leave them with at least a couple of specific actions that they could keep moving forward with—and to leave them feeling empowered to do so.

My goal here is to do the same—to share the specific, actionable steps you can take to:

- live your authentic personal brand
- move the needle of your independent consulting business towards your goals
- earn the income you know you've earned

I hope to help you create a life of design.

"This [content] provides practical, real-world, easy-to-apply approaches and tactics that are useful for both new and highly experienced consultants. Much of this content is equally valuable for internal consultants. As a result...I have all I need to rev-up my plan to take my craft as a consultant to the next level."

- TRACEY SCOTT, PIPELINE REGULATORY CONSULTANT

BUYER'S BONUS

As a way of saying thank you for your purchase, I'm offering a free cheat sheet to download.

>>> Go to www.tanyastevenson.com/report

This cheat sheet covers the following topics to help you build your independent consulting business:

- **Goal Setting**—focus on what you need to do to create a successful business and architect the life you want
- **Mindset**—shift your paradigm to help you take action to move your business and yourself to the next level
- **Personal Branding and Specialization**—target your ideal clients and stand out in the market
- **Marketing and Lead Generating**—set yourself up to have your choice of multiple opportunities, when *you* want them
- **Types of Contracts and Setting Terms**—position yourself and your contract for the best outcome possible
- **Negotiate**—with confidence

...and much, much more.

"[Tanya's Program] is a comprehensive introduction to creating a meaningful pathway forward to building a successful business. The presentation and material are well thought-out, organized, and impactful. Tanya is very good at bringing a large amount of information, distilling it down to what is most important to know and how to apply it. I moved from a mindset of overwhelmed to a mindset of inspiration and creation. My next steps are manageable, understandable and actionable. The magic to all of this work is Tanya's wisdom, experience, and natural ability to bring the content to life. I am empowered and ready to take my next steps in building a business to serve and make the world a better place."

- JESSICA SCHNEIDER, WELLTH COACHING AND CONSULTING

HOW TO USE THIS BOOK

The reality is that anyone can pick up and read this book—but not everyone will see the results. The difference between the consultant who improves her personal brand and the guy who just buys another book is one simple thing: **taking action**.

To get the most out of this book, I encourage you to do three things:

1. Have an open mind so you can accept new ideas.
2. Implement the strategies that you learn as you're reading.
3. Take what works and discard what doesn't.

Apply what you learn and tweak it to make it your own, and implement it bit by bit over time.

"Absorb what is useful, reject what is useless, add what is specifically your own." – Bruce Lee, Martial Artist. *Bruce Lee—Wisdom for the Way*

Don't overthink it; let it flow

When it comes to acting on the suggestions in this book, the trick is to not take a lot of time—don't overthink it. Read each chapter and try to apply the content as you go, then continue reading.

This is a process, and each chapter builds upon the previous one. Once you have finished the book, go back and rework the content.

I still repeat many of the steps in this book yearly.

This isn't a test—your first answer doesn't have to be right. You will find you will need to take action, implement the steps, test the outputs, and then update.

Wash—rinse—repeat

If you do this, I promise your professional life will transform and you'll attain the rewards of your authentic personal brand and the independent consulting business you've always wanted.

THIS BOOK IS DEDICATED TO ALL MY PREVIOUS MENTEES, STUDENTS, AND CLIENTS

You are the reason why I do what I do. I am honoured to play a small role in your career development and independent consulting businesses.

I also want to dedicate this book to my husband and family who have supported my unconventional journey. Chris, Kathy and Bernie, Laurie and Cathy, Natasha, Rhonda, Cindy and Daniel—thank you for believing in me.

Let's not forget the friends who have inspired me to keep going during tough moments: Tara, Juan, Valerie, Carol, Jane, Ernest, Janice, and Sylvia. Some of you have been there since the beginning, and others have joined me for my more recent adventures. Regardless—I'm grateful beyond words for your support and for being there when I need you.

I want to give a particular, heartfelt call-out to my friend and Marketing Strategist, Myke Macapinlac. You helped me zero-in on my calling to help my fellow consultants. Plus, you convinced me it was the right time to write this third book as my way to give back. Thank you Myke, for being who you are, for caring about me and my passion for business, and for doing all that you do.

DISCLAIMER

I've verified the information in this book as best I can, but differing opinions obviously exist. Neither the publisher nor I assume legal responsibility for any omissions or contrary interpretations of the content.

This book is based on my experience, and the views I have shared should not be taken as commands. The reader is responsible for his or her own actions.

The people described in this book are real, but I've changed their names to protect their confidentiality.

Table of Contents

Chapter 1 1
   What is Personal Branding? 1

Chapter 2 6
   The Importance and Benefits of Personal Branding 6

Chapter 3 12
   Common Mistakes and Myths About Personal Branding 12

Chapter 4 27
   Questions to Reveal Your Authentic Personal Brand 27

Chapter 5 37
   How to Validate What Your Market Thinks About You 37

Chapter 6 43
   The Must-Have Tools for Building Your Personal Brand 43

Chapter 7 51
   How to Amplify Your Influence and Demonstrate Your
   Authority 51

Chapter 8 64
   How to Network in Person 64

Chapter 9 87

How to Manage Your Reputation Effectively..................................87

Chapter 10 92

What Now? 92

CHAPTER 1

What is Personal Branding?

"Who are you?' said the Caterpillar. Alice replied, rather shyly, 'I—I hardly know, sir, just at present—at least I know who I WAS when I got up this morning, but I think I must have been changed several times since then.'" Lewis Carroll, *Alice's Adventures in Wonderland*

And there is the truth of the matter.

You have grown in many aspects of your life, both personally and professionally. As a result, you have changed, and you may not be fully aware of who you are today. You know what you have learned, done, accomplished, and contributed. You also likely know what you want going forward.

But are you fully aware of who YOU are, of what YOU have to offer as a professional or as an independent consultant, and of how YOU differ from your peers?

What the heck does Alice in Wonderland have to do with personal branding?

Personal branding is knowing the answers to those questions. You want to answer those questions for yourself so that the world can know the answers too. Otherwise, how can you live purposefully to get the life you want? And how can others help you get what you want? Knowing deeply who you are and what you represent, then communicating this through a personal brand is how great consultants connect to the world—and how the world connects to them.

"Branding is the art of becoming knowable, likable and trustable." – John Jantsch, Founder of Duct Tape Marketing

Let me give you an example

Like many of you, I grew up watching music and movie icons. One of my favourites from my generation was Madonna. I was not only fascinated by her music and sense of style, but by the way she managed her career and business.

From very early on, Madonna was in control of her look and her presentation. She realised she was a business and developed herself as a brand. As a result, her successful career and various business offerings have stood the test of time—*all based on her personal brand.*

"A lot of people are afraid to say what they want. That's why they don't get it." – Madonna, American singer-songwriter and producer often referred to as the 'Queen of Pop'

What we can all learn from my controversial idol: a personal brand is essential

Why is it essential? A personal brand is the only thing you're going to have that is truly *all yours*. And how you express your brand, especially digitally in the new business world, is important in this new age. We live in a time where you can't hide yourself. So help your business stand the test of time, and build your brand.

"A brand is the set of expectations, memories, stories, and relationships that, taken together, account for a consumer's decision to choose one product or service over another." – Seth Godin, author of *Linchpin* and founder of the altMBA

To attain their true value, personal brands need to represent our authentic selves

Openly demonstrating our strengths, values, abilities, and experiences is what sets us apart from others in our field. Our unique combination is what shows clients why they should choose to work with *us*, and this furthers our careers and businesses as independent consultants.

"It's important to build a personal brand because it's the only thing you're going to have. Your reputation online and in the new business world is pretty much the game, so you've got to be a good person. You can't hide anything, and more importantly, you've got to be out there at some level." – Gary Vaynerchuk, author of *Crush It! And CEO of VoynerX*

Personal brand is how to attract the clients you want, not conform to the clients you get

You've got to be out there so you can move towards your goals—with *the right clients.* You're only human. You're not going to be for everyone. That's the reality: there are people who aren't your tribe. And that's not only okay; it's what you want. Personal branding is differentiating. When you have differentiated yourself consistently over time, you will find *your* tribe and preferred clients more easily.

"Branding demands commitment: commitment to continual re-invention; striking chords with people to stir their emotions; and commitment to imagination. It is easy to be cynical about such things, much harder to be successful." – Sir Richard Branson, CEO of Virgin

I am now comfortable saying "I'm not for everyone"

Thankfully, I have built my business to the point where I can say this. Why is that not scary? Thanks to my brand, I am *exactly* what many people in my network are looking for, and they demonstrate it consistently by:

- hiring me to consult with them or to coach them or their team
- referring me to those in their network who need my services and style
- asking for my advice
- following my online content and comment

The remainder of this book will provide the steps I use to position myself to promote my personal brand, and consequently, my consulting services. These steps help me attract my ideal clients and contract opportunities.

"People do not buy goods and services. They buy relations, stories and magic." – Seth Godin

CHAPTER 2

The Importance and Benefits of Personal Branding

Are you still unpersuaded?

"Personal branding? Why would I worry about that? I'm a consultant; my work speaks for itself."

Sound like you? Well, you may be doing yourself a disservice. Let me make my case:

You have been working away in your consulting career for some time now. You deliver excellent results. Your clients love working with you. Yet, when the budget runs out when clients are scarce, you struggle to find your next engagement.

Fabulous consultants + personal brand = more success

I have seen this outcome again and again when fabulous consultants don't make any effort to promote their personal brand. They have great value to offer, yet they do not stand out next to others who provide the same services. And even when they stand out, they aren't able to negotiate the rates and terms that reflect the value they bring.

"The right kind of branding will get you noticed, remembered, and hired by the people you want to be hired by." – Unknown

I have observed 5 specific reasons independent consultants need to take personal branding more seriously.

Reason 1: It actually applies to you

So many consultants believe branding is only applicable to brick and mortar, retail, or big corporations.

Not true. You have a brand…right now. Do you know what people think of you? What they are saying? How they are making decisions about you?

"Personal branding is about managing your name — even if you don't own a business — in a world of misinformation, disinformation, and semi-permanent Google records. Going on a date? Chances are that your "blind" date has Googled your name. Going to a job interview? Ditto." – Tim Ferriss, entrepreneur, public speaker, and author of *4-Hour Work Week*

I wouldn't be where I am had I not learned this lesson early

I am very grateful to have learned this lesson early in my career. I learned it because I hired a career coaching firm (at an extreme cost) that drilled the concept into my head. I know that if I hadn't done that, I would have progressed a heck of a lot more slowly in my career, and my transition to consulting would have been more difficult.

For those who haven't received this valuable branding advice…Not having a personal brand restricts your freedom to choose your own engagements and leaves you with only what is available at the time.

"Loyalty is not won by being first. It is won by being best."
– Unknown

Reason 2: You attract the right clients

Did you become a consultant because you wanted to choose your clients? Do you still need to work with difficult clients?

When I first started, I couldn't be picky about my clients. But because I had a strong brand when I stepped out, I seemed to have fewer difficult clients than some of my peers. That is another excellent reason to build, maintain, and continue to grow your brand—it helps you attract the clients you *want to work with*.

"If people like you, they will listen to you, but if they trust you, they'll do business with you." – Zig Ziglar, salesman, motivational speaker, and author of *Secretes of Closing the Sale*

When you can attract the clients and team you want to work with, you can do your true work—the work that you are excited to get up in the morning to do.

"Your brand is a gateway to your true work. You know you are here to do something – to create something or help others in some way. The question is, how can you set up your life and work so that you can do it? The answer lies in your brand. When you create a compelling brand, you attract people who want the promise of your brand – which you deliver." – Dave Buck, CEO of CoachVille

<u>Reason 3: Clients take you seriously</u>

Who doesn't want to be taken seriously?

If you want to help your clients and want them to consider your ideas, then yes, you want to be taken seriously.

Having a strong brand helps you work towards a collaborative working relationship with your client. It means you can help them make the right changes to resolve the problems they have hired you to solve.

Which sets you up for the next reason…

Reason 4: You increase trust faster with your clients and stakeholders

When you are taken more seriously, you can build trust with your clients and stakeholders faster.

A great consultant can build trust, but to grow it faster is a value-add.

For example, my strong personal brand means people know who I am, and this means we can move our attention to the problem and solution more quickly, rather than being distracted by my addition to the team. I am all for finding ways to reduce the noise from and resistance to my presence.

This has always added value in my ability to negotiate. When my peers recognise my brand, my reputation precedes me, and they are very comfortable advocating on my behalf. It means I am positioned for a realistic and honest conversation regarding my value rate.

Which leads to my last reason consultants should take branding more seriously…

Reason 5: You can make more money

"If you are not a brand, you are a commodity." – Philip Kotler, S.C. Johnson & Son Professor of International Marketing at the Kellogg™ School of Management, Northwestern University

What more do I have to say? That's a good reason right there.

The biggest takeaway here is that you have a brand, and you need to take it seriously. Once you genuinely own your brand and take steps to manage it, you are well on your way to receiving the rewards.

> "This [personal branding content] really allowed me to see I have a lot of work to do to position myself in the market and to become known for what it is that I can offer. In a lot of ways, I have been going through the motions without intentionality, which I need to apply to be successful...The most valuable aspects [was] gained during the Personal Branding & Specialization topics."
>
> **- GREG KANTOR, BUSINESS ANALYST CONSULTANT**

CHAPTER 3

Common Mistakes and Myths About Personal Branding

Are you still skeptical about personal branding? Perhaps debunking some common myths will help.

Many of my peers know I am a big advocate for personal branding. And they see the rewards I earn…is there a direct correlation between the two?

I was an early believer in the value of managing and building my personal brand. I liked it because it aligned well with one of my values: integrity. I developed a bit of a passion and dove into the research. Luckily, I wasn't persuaded by the common myths that often convince consultants not to invest in a personal brand.

These myths continue to do damage to great consultants. In this chapter I will debunk some of the most widespread myths and mistakes.

Myth/ Mistake 1: Creating an image is required to have a personal brand

Authenticity is the foundation of an effective personal brand. If you try to create spin, or an image that only applies to a particular aspect of your life, you will fail.

"Too many [people] want their brands to reflect some idealised, perfected image of themselves. As a consequence, their brands acquire no texture, no character and no public trust." – Sir Richard Branson

When I first started working, I got the suits that were expected, wore my hair as expected, and had the predictable website and business cards.

I felt like I was constantly itching and scratching. I was not comfortable in my own skin because it wasn't my skin. As a result, I was continuously questioning myself and eroding my confidence. I was losing bits of myself as the months passed and becoming exhausted by playing a role that wasn't really me.

The truth is, people can detect 'fake'—and they don't want anything to do with it.

"The most exhausting thing you can be is inauthentic." – Anne Morrow Lindbergh, author and aviation pioneer

Suddenly, I saw the mistake I was making. I realised that I value integrity, both in myself and in others, above many of my other values. Because I was learning to build and appreciate genuine connections with my network, I knew they could only be built on truth. So I started revealing my authentic 'image' instead of creating one I thought others wanted to see.

Once I stopped putting on a mask and started to be myself, my best self, my career and business really moved forward.

"The goal is to do business with people that believe what you believe." – Simon Sinek, motivational speaker and author of *Start With Why*

Myth/ Mistake 2: Assuming personal branding is just for large firms or famous people

Yes, corporations have brands, and famous people have personal brands. However, having a personal brand isn't necessarily a by-product of being famous.

Personal branding is something you already have, but usually are not conscious of. When you become more aware of your personal brand and decide you want to leverage it, then you can choose selectively how you want to build it and expose the areas in which you are 'famous'.

"All of us need to understand the importance of branding. We are CEOs of our own companies: Me Inc. To be in business today, our most important job is to be head marketer for the brand called You." – Tom Peters, author of *In Search of Excellence*

To do that, you need to understand how the people you want to connect with and influence will see you, and how to be ever-present to those people. The rest of the world doesn't have to know you even exist. You need to help the people you want to attract and interact with to find you where they are by focusing your efforts on them.

Myth/ Mistake 3: Thinking personal branding is expensive— both in money and time

One of the biggest myths out there is that building a brand takes a lot of time and money. This is understandable in the context of stories about corporations, political parties, and even famous people and how they built their brands.

As independent consultants, we are very much aware of the relationship between time and income. I have seen many of my peers hesitate to spend money. And I have seen even more of them hesitate to spend time on their personal brand over work they could bill their clients for.

"Stopping [branding] to save money is like stopping your watch to save time." – Henry Ford, founder of the Ford Motor Company

But you show your branding with every email you write, comment you leave on LinkedIn, phone conversation you have, and meeting you facilitate—what does that cost? Being visible to decision makers by sharing your thoughts and demonstrating your abilities (*showing* not *telling*) is part of everything you do.

When you make every communication an opportunity to align with your personal brand, then you are working on your personal brand daily, if not hourly, with no money involved and barely any additional time.

Now, imagine what you could accomplish if you invested just an hour or two a week in showing your potential clients what you can do to solve their problems. Would that be a fair trade of time and money to help build your business?

"There is no greater agony than bearing an untold story inside you." – Maya Angelou, author and activist

Myth/ Mistake 4: Thinking personal branding and boasting are synonymous

People often think that personal branding is about telling as many people as possible how great they are.

Now, I am not against doing some self-promotion. And if you are a female independent consultant, I would suggest checking in and asking if you are doing enough to promote yourself.

However, there's a difference between 'telling' everyone how great you are and 'showing' them. And that's where promoting yourself can go wrong.

"Depending on what they are, our habits will either make us or break us." – Sean Covey, President of FranklinCovey Education

The most crucial part of personal branding is the 'showing'

Personal branding is more about demonstrating what makes you *you*. Showing what makes you great in all that you do—every day—is a more effective strategy than telling, by far. One especially valuable way to do this is to show your client how you can solve their problems.

"Sell the problem you solve, not the product." – Unknown

When you 'show,' it is authentic, and your brand will be held in the hearts and minds of those who know you. They, in turn, will advocate for you, which will help spread your brand.

But *how* do you 'show'?

Don't worry—I'll provide more in chapter 7.

Myth/ Mistake 5: Separating personal branding from professional branding

Now that I am more comfortable with my personal brand and have experienced the rewards of being authentic in all aspects of my life, I don't see a difference between my personal and professional brand.

Of course, my personal brand has shifted over time. When I was younger, I was extremely sensitive to pain inflicted on others and animals, brutally honest, openly rebellious against institutions, and extremely hard working.

These roots of who I am showed up differently with my family than with my classmates or my co-workers. But over time, as I have become more authentic and more me, I demonstrate the same qualities in both my personal and professional life.

They are one and the same to me.

"There is no professional or personal anymore. There's simply your brand. Everything you do affects your brand, and it's up to you to determine whether your brand is affected positively or negatively. That's it." – Peter Shankman, author and founder of HARO

I know many independent consultants believe there is a hard line, if not a tall wall, between their real world branding and their virtual world activities. For example, they may behave differently at an in person networking or speaking event than in their online published content like their blogs, LinkedIn articles, or comments in professional discussion groups.

But I have experienced more efficient use of my time and more effective results by linking the real and virtual worlds. I build authentic relationships with my network by consistently acting, speaking, and behaving the same way across all my channels of interaction and communication. That way, I send a consistent message while amplifying my visibility and reducing the effort required to build an ever-growing personal brand.

Myth/ Mistake 6: Placing too much emphasis on word of mouth and referrals

Most independent consultants will attain their first, second, and even third contract due to word-of-mouth referrals. And this is a critical part of your lead-generating or business development strategy. However, it can't be your only 'tool' to attain opportunities.

The risk of depending *solely* on this strategy is that your peers' understanding of who you are and what you bring (and thus the kinds of projects to which they refer you for,) may not align with where you want to take your business.

For example, a senior consultant I admire noticed that her advocates were continually referring her for opportunities that only used a fraction of her potential. During our discussion of her concern it became apparent to her that she had not invested enough in managing her personal brand. As a result, her fans (who were trying to be helpful) kept suggesting her for opportunities for which she did great work, but not the work she wanted to do. But once she started clearly articulating her new personal brand, her fans were more than happy to help her find her ideal clients and opportunities.

On that note, I recommend you apply multiple ways to spread the word about your personal brand. In doing so, you will be more independent and in control of your business as a consultant.

Myth/ Mistake 7: Believing it's better to hide behind your service representative brand than to promote your own

When I was an employed leader and decision maker, I often worked with vendors who provided various services. One of the most important was the one that helped me find great consultants to help solve my organisation's problems. In turn, I provided recommendations and testimonials to the vendors I felt did a great job, to help them build their businesses.

So, the same vendors I used when I was a employed leader then became my service representatives when I first started my business as an independent consultant. I knew the value of having them help me promote my services. I recognised that without their assistance, it would be hard to move my business forward. I quickly figured out how to co-brand with those same vendors, and the advantages for both of us created a win-win-win situation for my potential clients, my service representatives, and myself.

Some independent consultants depend solely on the vendor's branding and reputation and keep their own as quiet as possible. They hope not to 'offend' their service representative by making it seem that potential clients would choose them over the service representative.

The problem with this is that, if you don't invest in your own branding, especially if you can deliver quality results that your clients appreciate, then you are limiting your *own* potential opportunities and revenue. You won't ever truly realise your own potential and will always be in someone else's shadow.

By co-branding, I have not only experienced business growth, but when I have done it respectfully, vendors are more than happy to help me because I have a strong, authentic personal brand.

Myth/ Mistake 8: Building your personal brand is selfish and narcissistic

Sure, there are consultants who portray these qualities, but there are plenty who do just the opposite.

There's the 'icky' brand...

When I have been 'turned off' by someone's personal brand, I may not be able to put my finger on the 'why' at first. But, upon reflection, it's usually when I sense that the consultant is pushing themselves solely to advance their business rather than to share how they can genuinely help their clients—that becomes 'icky'.

And there's the authentic brand...

The consultants or other service providers who think of their brand as a way to deliver value to others and contribute to their client's success in a unique style—they are far more successful. These consultants approach their brand from a place of generosity, service, and capability—not from selfishness.

"Don't be ashamed of your story. It will inspire others." – Amy Rees Anderson, founder of REES Capital

When you think about your brand as a way to achieve your personal mission in support of others, you'll be confident in building it—confident, not arrogant.

Myth/ Mistake 9: Thinking online personal branding is only for influencers

There was a time where I didn't take action to help myself because I didn't think I deserved the results, or that I hadn't earned the 'right'. I perceived social media and other digital channels as being reserved for influencers, and I wasn't one yet.

But denying yourself the same tools that popular influencers use just because you think you're not popular enough doesn't make sense. It doesn't matter who you are, what job title you have, or what your career goals are: you need to have a digital brand that shows that you're a player in today's world of work— a brand that conveys the authentic individual whom people would meet if they connected with you offline.

So when I looked at my successful role models and the tools they used, I found ways to apply similar approaches for myself and my goals. And, well, let's just say I was rewarded too.

Your brand has moved online too, and you need to manage it the same way you manage your brand in the real world.

Myth/ Mistake 10: Waiting to brand yourself until you need it tomorrow

If you plan to wait to focus on your personal brand until you're just about to finish your last contract or are between contracts, think again.

Waiting until you're done your last contract and in need of another is not the ideal time to be focused on your personal brand. If anything, it may be more of a distraction and frustrating for both yourself and your potential new clients.

This is a classic issue with personal branding, and I understand why it occurs.

As a consultant who delivers results, you may find yourself fully committed to your client. And like many others out there, you might not have much energy to focus on helping yourself once your work day ends.

But to really reap the rewards of managing your personal brand, you can't afford to focus your business attention 100% on the client right in front of you and on yourself only when you are not on contract.

When you make this mistake, you are acting more like an employee, not like a business looking out for its goals.

If you continue to wait, I guarantee you will be on the bench, or on it longer than you want to be.

"The best time to plant a tree was 10 years ago. The second best time is today." – Chinese proverb

Myth/ Mistake 11: Believing you can do it on your own

There are aspects of your personal brand that you can and should handle on your own. But there are also things you need for your personal branding that will require expertise you may not have. We'll highlight these in Chapter 7, **How to Amplify Your Influence and Demonstrate Your Authority**.

This reminds me of my first business card and website. They were fine for what I needed at the time. But because I was not a graphic artist, I didn't understand how the colours I'd chosen would translate on the paper I chose, and the website was cumbersome for those who were visiting for the first time.

But as my business grew, I recognised opportunities where it just made more sense to hire help. And in doing so, I helped myself stay aligned with what my personal brand was becoming known for—delivering results to those I care about.

The moral of the story...

It's time to ditch the personal branding myths and start advancing your career and business. The reality is that effective personal branding comes naturally and is easily woven into corporate branding and the daily business of life, online and offline.

CHAPTER 4

Questions to Reveal Your Authentic Personal Brand

An authentic brand is easy to honour, live by, and deliver daily

It takes courage and patience to be clear about your brand, but putting in the work to be authentic will cost you less in the long run. Because an authentic brand is one that is *you*, it's easy to sustain and maintain, which will make it easier for you to differentiate yourself in your market.

"As an entrepreneur, one of the biggest challenges you will face will be building your brand. The ultimate goal is to set your company and your brand apart from the crowd. If you form a strategy without doing the research, your brand will barely float – and at the speed industries move at today, brands sink fast." – Ryan Holmes, founder and CEO of Hootsuite

How did I come to these realisations?

Early in my career, my confidence had taken a blow. I was extremely fortunate that my husband and I had invested in a career coach at the time. The coaching process introduced me to the need to be introspective and to be receptive to vital external feedback.

It was great timing, as I was also doing some serious reflecting on where I had come from and where I wanted to go. To further my self-reflection, my career coach had me do a serious overhaul of my resume.

The coach suggested I take the time to write down 200 accomplishments, along with what it took to achieve them (skills, capabilities, support, etc.). I also had to include the positive results or impact that came from them—either in my life or for others.

200?! Yes, that many.

Thankfully, they didn't all have to be work-related (though, to be honest, the work-related ones were easy). I also added personal accomplishments from volunteering, from my community involvement, and from my family life. Then the coach asked me a bunch of questions to make me dig even deeper.

The rewards from this exercise were exceptional

The clarity I gained about who I was, what inspired and motivated me, and what I wanted (not only for my career but for my life) was, well, life-changing. I will always be grateful, not only for the service, but for the career coach.

The biggest lessons I took away were:

- We have all made a difference—far more than we realize.
- We shouldn't be afraid to get to know ourselves; we're worth it.
- We can use reflection as a tool to free ourselves.
- We can all use help to reveal our value, our brand.
- We are the only ones who can genuinely reveal and live our authentic brand.

"It's not about being different, it's about the difference you make." – Karl D. Speak & David McNally, authors of *Be Your Own Brand*

The right questions are valuable tools to help you unveil and describe your brand. Here are questions to ask yourself:

Questions to reflect on your values

Values are what is important to you. Values aren't what you say they are; you demonstrate them by how you feel, behave, and react. They guide your daily decisions and actions, either consciously or unconsciously. When you act with your values, you are confident, energised, motivated, and more readily available to others.

The first step in reflecting on your brand is to know what your real values are and what blocks you from living in harmony with them.

Your reflection questions for your values are:

1. What are the three activities you spend the most time on? Not the activities you think you *should be doing*—where does your time *really go*? To find out, just track your activities for a week. It will quickly become obvious.
2. What situations make you feel annoyed, frustrated, or even angry?

"You have to understand your own personal DNA. Don't do things because I do them or Steve Jobs or Mark Cuban tried it. You need to know your personal brand and stay true to it." – Gary Vaynerchuk

Questions to reflect on your passions

Identifying your passions tell you about what motivates you. Your passions infuse you with energy, and this is what attracts others to your network. When you are clear about your passions, you can find ways to make them part of your brand.

Your reflection questions for your passions are:

3. What aspects of your consulting craft do you love the most?
4. What topics can you talk about easily and endlessly?
5. What activities do you get excited or animated about doing?

"I've come to believe that each of us has a personal calling that's as unique as a fingerprint—and that the best way to succeed is to discover what you love and then find a way to offer it to others in the form of service, working hard, and also allowing the energy of the universe to lead you." – Oprah Winfrey, media executive, actor, and philanthropist

Questions to reflect on your most significant strengths

Your greatest strengths are the capabilities or skills you have that your peers may not. They are another foundational aspect of who you are. Usually, these advantages are readily available to you, and you use them effortlessly. Because they are so easy for you to use, they may not be obvious to you. So it is even more vital for you to reflect on them and to define them clearly.

Your reflection questions for your strengths are:

6. What do your clients or peers tell you that you do well?
7. What tasks or activities come easily to you?
8. What approach or tool do you apply no matter what service or product you're contracted to provide?

"Promote your strengths. Remind the world why you are special and why it is special to do business with you." – Mary Schnack, communications specialist and President of Mary Schnack & Associates

Questions to reflect on your personality

What parts of yourself can you bring to your clients? Look at the previous questions and your brainstormed answers—they're related. When I reflect on this question, I believe I bring my energy, enthusiasm, can-do attitude, and the reasons why I have this attitude. I show my positive outlook by sharing stories from my past and exceptional results from projects I have been honoured to be part of.

Your reflection questions for your personality are:

9. What aspects of your character help you persevere in tough situations?
10. What aspects of your personality seem to help you stand out to your clients?

"Your smile is your logo, your personality is your business card, how you leave others feeling after having an experience with you becomes your trademark." – Jay Danzie, brand strategist

Questions to reflect on your differentiators

Often clients want to treat independent consultants as a commodity and not as a valuable partner. Your brand needs to represent your differentiating aspects so that you stand out at the same time as you act authentically. Understanding and capitalising on your differentiators means you can attract your ideal clients who choose you *for you*.

Your reflection questions for your differentiators are:

11. What do you think most strongly sets you apart from your peer consultants?
12. Why do you think your clients have chosen you over others?

"Be bold, and original. Tell 'em something that they don't know" – Melinda Emerson, author of *Become Your Own Boss in 12 Months*

Questions to reflect on your target niche and market

Delivering products or services that address the needs of a particular group has multiple benefits. This:

- reduces your competition
- increases your knowledge of your preferred clients
- improves your marketing efficiency

If you haven't yet reflected on your target market

Don't worry, you have been targeting throughout your working years. It doesn't matter if you were an employee or a consultant—all your experience is a history for you to reflect on. Look back at where you were most successful, enjoyed your work most, and applied your skills and craft. This will help you determine where you want to focus your personal brand moving forward.

Your reflection questions for your target niche and market are:

13. In which particular market have you applied your skills most successfully?
14. What type of problems do your clients come to you to solve?
15. Where have you seen solutions that others haven't?

"Want to build your brand? Focus on the group of folks that love you and let go of the rest." – Marcus Sheridan, web marketing expert and author of *They Ask, You Answer*

Questions to reflect on your purpose

Your purpose is the other pillar of your authentic brand. When you have clarity of purpose or mission, you are clear about how you want to contribute to the world beyond your career as a consultant. Your purpose also acts as a compass for your decisions and tells you what opportunities to avoid.

Your reflection questions for your purpose are:

16. If you won the lottery and didn't need to work, where would you focus your time?
17. What is your biggest hope or dream for you, your family, or your community?

Questions to reflect on your consulting craft

As a Change Management and Leadership Transformation consultant, I strive to clarify what behaviours (for leaders and their teams,) need to change to achieve the desired outcomes, and I am aware of the unique experiences, tactics, and education that I bring to deliver these results.

For example, the experience I gained implementing change as a department leader gave me insights I now apply to change management. My education has taught me the theory, and my personal and professional experiences have taught me the real-life tactics. I use it all in my consulting craft and in articulating my brand.

Your reflection questions for your consulting craft are:

18. Why do you consult?
19. What do you hope will be the result of your work as a consultant?
20. What value do you promise to deliver during your engagement?

"If you show up regularly with generosity, everything else is gonna take care of itself." – Seth Godin

Now that you have taken the time to answer these questions, it's time to discover how the external world has seen you demonstrate your personal brand.

CHAPTER 5

How to Validate What Your Market Thinks About You

Chapter 4 revealed the questions to ask yourself to help clarify your authentic personal brand. Now I invite you to embark on the adventure of asking questions of others and reflecting on their answers. Will they match?

Why bother, you ask?

Your network has observed your behaviours, which have left an impression. Talking to trusted individuals in your network, who have been with you in both personal and professional situations, can provide meaningful feedback about how they interpret your behaviours.

It will be vital to be open to receive feedback and to be introspective. But don't worry, it's worth the courage and patience.

At first it takes some getting used to

Once I had a meeting with two trusted people from my network whom I also consider friends. Carol described my underlying approach to my work to Valerie, and she called me "violently organized".

The truth is that when I first heard this statement, I instantly rebelled against the term "violently". This word raised negative emotions in me. But because I was curious and asked Carol what she meant, I learned it was a compliment and that Carol was often in awe of how well-organised I was in my work.

If I tried to avoid being myself—violently organized—I would actually hurt myself and create more chaos for myself. However, Carol's statement also helped me realise that I needed to manage my one strength with another: being flexible when the situation requires it.

So instead of denying the feedback, I decided to claim it—to own it

I decided to integrate the feedback into my personal brand as one of my key strengths and a differentiator for my craft as a consultant. Change managers are often seen as fluffy and soft. Nope, not me. I deliver results with a blend of violent organisation and flexibility in the face of change and unexpected outcomes.

So, on that note, I would suggest finding 6 individuals you trust—3 from personal circumstances and 3 from professional situations—who have spent considerable time with you and whom you know will give you honest and constructive input.

Are you ready to ask your trusted network some great questions and get feedback for your personal brand?

Remember, there are no 'right' answers. There may be some you agree with and some you don't, but every answer will help you define how you want to demonstrate your authentic personal brand moving forward.

Questions to ask your network to reveal your values:

1. What are the three activities on which you see me spend the most time?
2. In what situations have you seen me seem flustered, annoyed, or even angry?

Questions to ask your network to reveal your passions:

3. What aspects of my consulting work do I seem to love the most?
4. What topics can I talk about easily and endlessly?

5. What activities do I get excited or animated about doing?

Questions to ask your network to reveal your strengths:

6. What have you observed or heard friends, colleagues, or clients say that I've done well?

7. What tasks or activities do you think come easily to me?

8. What approach or tool have you seen me use in most situations, no matter what service or product I'm contracted to provide?

Questions to ask your network to reveal your personality:

9. What aspects of my character seem to help me persevere in tough situations?

10. What aspects of my character make me stand out to you or to others?

Questions to ask your network to reveal your differentiators:

11. What do you believe sets me apart from my peer consultants?

12. What do you think my clients or teammates appreciate about me over others?

Questions to ask your network to reveal your target niche and market:

13. In which markets have you seen me apply my skills most successfully?
14. What services or products do you think I provide?
15. How would you describe what I do for others and how I go about it?

Questions to ask your network to reveal your demonstrated purpose:

16. What problems would you seek me out to solve for or with you?
17. Why do you think I consult?
18. What do you think I would pursue if money were no issue?

<u>And when you're done...</u>

You now have a wealth of information to sift through. You can reflect on the answers your network provided to get valuable insight on how to shape your personal brand. This process requires that you discover and come to know your 'real' self—both how you see yourself and how others see you—before you can express your authentic brand with your peers, clients, and your community.

If you already have a coach or close mentor, I would suggest you involve them in your reflection process. Having an external person to both ask you the questions in Chapter 5 and review the answers from Chapter 6 is an effective way to gain a clear, objective perspective. I can't express enough the value of having a coach with me through this experience—it has been life-changing.

A final task

Take a moment and search for yourself on the Internet and review the results. Do they reflect what you've just learned from yourself and others?

"Your brand is your public identity, what you're trusted for. And for your brand to endure, it has to be tested, redefined, managed, and expanded as markets evolve. Brands either learn or disappear." – Lisa Gansky, co-founder and CEO of Global Network Navigator

CHAPTER 6

The Must-Have Tools for Building Your Personal Brand

Now that you've consciously articulated and crafted your authentic personal brand, it's a question of getting it out there so others know about it too.

But don't worry…

New ways to connect with clients are waiting just around the corner

There are multiple channels, using multiple mediums, that you can use to network and provide value to improve your personal brand. You're probably thinking: this sounds extremely time-consuming. And how much money do I need?

But the truth is, it doesn't have to be time-consuming or expensive. Yes, some effort is required. But all you have to do is plan ahead and ensure you provide value.

"Invest in yourself. You can afford it. Trust me." – Rashon Carraway, founder and Chief LifeStyle Operator of Rashon Carraway Designs

It's not like the olden days where there were only two "new" ways

At the beginning of my career, there were really only two worthy platforms from which to express yourself.

There was the Internet where you could (more or less) hang your virtual shingle. [From stage left—old geezer enters and says in an old person voice…] Back in my day, this was not a friendly medium for non-tech individuals. Unless you were used to coding and knew your way around programming, you pretty well had to hire a webpage programmer and designer.

Thankfully, today, there are many ways to create a website easily using various types of platforms. At the time of writing this book, those options include: using blogging sites or website builders like Wix, or even using the website-building service provided by your domain hosting company. Lucky you!

And then there was LinkedIn.

"LinkedIn is the world's largest professional network with hundreds of millions of members, and growing rapidly." – LinkedIn

I was an early adopter of LinkedIn, so I have watched the platform evolve over time.

Today, there are so many ways to express your personal brand. So many, in fact, that it may be difficult to know where to start, or, if you have started, where to go next.

"Start where you are. Use what you have. Do what you can." – Arthur Ashe, professional tennis player and winner of three Grand Slam titles

Let me save you some time. Here's what I've learned:

If I were to do it all over again, I would focus on the next 3 things, in order, to help me express my personal brand. The order is important because the content from one sets the foundation for the next. And if you have any of these set up already, this is the perfect time to review and freshen them up.

"Ask yourself if what you're doing today is getting you closer to where you want to be tomorrow." – Unknown

So let's get started…

1. **Attain and set up your own professional domain and email address**

    Your domain and address should align with how you want to be known—they're part of your brand.

    Free services are nice…but it also looks like you're doing things on the cheap. You don't want to exemplify the saying, "the shoemaker's children go barefoot" (the 'children' are your personal branding, your consulting craft, and your career or business).

    When I first started out, I wanted to be known as someone who would stand behind my word and deliver results. As a result, I started with the company name Stand & Deliver Inc. and the domain www.standanddeliverinc.com.

    Over time, and due to refreshing my personal brand, I have acquired additional domains and email addresses. I had the good fortune of purchasing the domain to match my name, www.tanyastevenson.com. I also have a shorter version of the domain for my company—because it's easier to say off-the-cuff and for potential clients to remember—as well as the email address to go with the domain www.stand-inc.com.

I have re-routed or forwarded these to land where I want. That is the beauty of refreshing your personal brand tools these days:

- you have options for how to keep track of what you have
- you can leverage the new addresses
- it gives you a 'fresh' look if you want to express a new and evolved personal brand to your network

So, if you already have a domain and email address, please don't think you have to start fresh.

"A domain name is your address, your address on the internet. We all have a physical address; we're all going to need an address in cyberspace. They're becoming increasingly important. I believe we'll get to the point where when you're born, you'll be issued a domain name." – Bob Parsons, founder of CEO of GoDaddy.com

Once you have a new or refreshed professional domain and email address you are ready for step 2.

2. **Create your own website, with a place to share your thoughts**

The thing to keep in mind here is: *get a website up* (even if you only have one page—your blog). Prove to the world you are a real person who provides real value in your market. A section called Articles, Blog, or My Thoughts is a **must have.** It's where you share valuable content with your peers and target clients.

You can always update and improve your website later, and you can commit a little or a lot of time to doing so. A next step would be to post your bio and a page that describes your services and products and the value and benefits you provide. The world needs to know about you!

3. **Ensure you have an up-to-date and professional LinkedIn profile**

Why bother with LinkedIn? Because it is THE professional networking tool out there, so there's no better medium to convey your brand. Mind you, I'm a little biased because I've been a LinkedIn user since it began in 2002. That being said, I think it has contributed greatly to my success because it is:

- a platform for your **professional** profile
- a place for you to share content, connect with others, and exchange ideas
- searchable, so your potential clients can find you

"How do you want the world to see you professionally? What kinds of work do you enjoy doing? Why are you on LinkedIn? Those are the questions you should think about when creating your LinkedIn profile, so it's aligned with your personal brand. While marketing-speak like 'personal brand' feels fake to many of us, we're really just talking about setting the right tone for your profile and positioning yourself for the kinds of opportunities you're interested in." — Melanie Pinola, author of *LinkedIn in 30 Minutes: How to create a rock-solid profile and build connections that matter*

Is your territory or market not a big user of LinkedIn?

Then find out where else your target market 'hangs out' online. For example, as I was writing, I searched "what are the LinkedIn alternatives in…" and added a target country or region. I found approximately 20 other alternatives. However, LinkedIn is still the primary professional online networking site for North America.

Now, you may be wondering, what's the difference between having your own website versus having a profile and using LinkedIn?

"A LinkedIn profile and a personal website serve two different purposes. Your LinkedIn profile should sum up your professional life and serves as a way to network with potential employers, clients, and associates. A personal website allows you to get a bit more creative – you can upload more images, have full control over aesthetics, and display more examples of your work. Both are useful to have in a competitive industry!" – Justin Belmont, founder and Editor-in-Chief of Prose Media

Some final thoughts

You can express your personal brand on LinkedIn, but you are limited to what LinkedIn allows. Your website is all yours. You are the creator of that domain. Enjoy the space: use it to add yet another layer about who you are and what problems you can help with, and to provide value that will attract your ideal network and clients.

"Creativity is intelligence having fun." –Joey Reiman, founder and Chairman of BrightHouse and author of *Thinking for a Living: Creating ideas that revitalize your business, career, and life*

So these are the first 3 steps to sharing your personal brand. They are foundational. Once you have these things in place, you will have a 'home' for all your online content and comments.

And that takes us to the next chapter, How you can amplify and demonstrate your authority (using these tools you have implemented as the medium).

CHAPTER 7

How to Amplify Your Influence and Demonstrate Your Authority

Are you wondering how you can demonstrate your abilities and build your authority within your network?

The first and most important effort we can make is to do a great job during our contracts—that's natural personal branding that speaks for itself. The second effort builds on the tools from the previous chapter—to *demonstrate* to your clients that you have the knowledge and ability to solve their problems. So when potential clients go looking for solutions to their problems, your content appears as the answer.

This chapter presents an active approach to personal branding: the practical things you can do to get your name, ability, and influence out there.

Above all, know your network's problems—and how to solve them

If you spend time learning about your network's problems and about how your target clients perceive them, you will be able to share useful content that will help them solve their problems.

"Personal Branding is all about your unique promise of value and what you bring to the table. It's [also] about getting your potential clients to choose you as the only solution to their problem." – Dr Sarah David, Associate Director, Mays Business School Career Management

An example from my own life

Earlier in my career, I often saw people struggling with their productivity. They were regularly disorganised, falling behind, missing deadlines, and disappointing people who were depending on them.

I struggled with understanding how so many of my peers and leaders could be so poor with their productivity. I had tamed that wild beast very early in my life—without even realising it—because I had no other choice.

I grew up in a rough environment. I aspired to thrive, not just survive. To do that, I needed to figure out how to have honour grades, hold down a job, help take care of my sister, and still have time to socialise in some way.

I naturally became very passionate about productivity—about finding ways to create shortcuts and be organised that resulted in repeatable systems.

I continued to apply these principles and learned new systems, tools and hacks throughout university and into my professional working career. In turn, I often moved ahead of my peers who hadn't yet figured out the same skills.

Eventually, people began to come to me for advice, and I, in turn, started to collect and share information I thought my peers would find helpful. This was everything from a book chapter or magazine article to a link to a tip on the net.

I would always ask myself: could this help someone in my network too?

As I found useful articles that helped me with my craft, my business, and my life in general, I would always ask who else I knew who might find them useful as well.

"Success has nothing to do with what you gain in life or accomplish for yourself. It's what you do for others." – Danny Thomas, actor, producer, and creator of *Make Room for Daddy*

This research was easy to do because it was already a passion of mine. I was reading all these different sources anyway—everything from business to productivity to my particular craft interests like psychology, sociology, processes, and project management. I also reviewed content related to marketing, digital graphics, art, and writing.

As time passed, more and more people asked, and I and kept helping. But to make it easier for me to help others, I started formatting the templates and quick how-to lists with my own personal touches. I would gather valuable content and stories, put it in an easily shareable and consumable format, and send it to my network of peers and clients.

My ideal clients not only appreciated the content, they shared it, which made them remember me for their next project.

"Start by knowing what you want and who you are, build credibility around it and deliver it online in a compelling way." – Krista Neher, author and CEO of Boot Camp Digital

That's how I approached helping others without having to put a lot of time and money into it. I figured out the topics I can research endlessly that are helpful not only to me but to others in my network. That is the value of some of the questions in chapter

5 and 6: they help you figure out what you can talk about endlessly.

And that is the trick: create content that is useful to others because it is related to their problems. The solutions can be related to your services and/ or products. You can also share insights and solutions from others, which shows you are confident and able to work with colleagues.

"Try not to become a man of success, but rather try to become a man of value." – Albert Einstein, theoretical physicist

Share your expertise to build your personal brand

There are multiple ways of sharing your or others' content and insights. Here are the 11 I practice. I encourage you to think about how you might incorporate them into your brand and work habits.

1. **Collect content that helps your clients and prepare it for easy sharing**

   I've already mentioned how I've gone about this. I've also gone as far as to leave my first book, *Rock Your Review: 10 Tips to Prove Your Performance*, as a gift for a client who was struggling with preparing for their performance review.

   Did it make a difference?

Yes. They, in turn, have given me testimonials, referred potential new clients, and re-contracted me later on.

I've seen others take this as far as to give a client a subscription to a magazine that was industry-related but had nothing do with the consulting service they provided.

The fun in this approach: it doesn't have to correlate directly to your own service offering. It could just be content that would be useful to your target market clients.

Actually, it can often be beneficial to share content that does not relate directly to your services because it demonstrates that you're looking out for your clients but don't expect anything in return. Indeed, this is the definition of a gift.

"Never get tired of doing little things for others. Sometimes those little things occupy the biggest part of their hearts." – Unknown

2. **Create content to help your target clients solve their problems**

In this case, try to relate the content to the issues you feel you can help with. That way, you are more efficient by applying what you are learning to what you are offering.

You can do this by writing articles or by creating easy free tools and sharing them on your website.

"Either write things worth reading or do things worth the writing." – Benjamin Franklin

3. **Post your own articles on LinkedIn**

This is how you can show depth and give a sense of who you are and what you're about in a popular, searchable medium.

"Thought leadership happens when you're willing to have your brand stand for more than what you sell." – Seth Price, keynote speaker and co-author of *The Road to Recognition*

4. **Join the conversation on LinkedIn or other forums**

Share useful content from others in your network or links to the content you've been collecting.

Did you happen to catch that quote I included earlier about the value of having both a website and a LinkedIn profile? It was from Justin Belmont, and I found it on the Quora forum. Justin provides content writing services. I noticed him because I was looking for a quote to help me express the concept. He offered me value. In turn, I looked him up and inquired about his services.

That's why you may want to join the conversation. If someone values your comments, those few words may be all it takes to attract a potential client.

"Active participation on LinkedIn is the best way to say, 'Look at me!' without saying 'Look at me!" – Bobby Darnell, founder and Principal of Construction Market Consultants

5. **Have a Twitter account**

Use your Twitter account at networking events, conferences, and seminars. Posting entertaining and useful content is a great way to attract followers.

I've used Twitter to have many post-conference follow-up conversations, and these conversations have led to exciting opportunities.

"Apart from creating a vibrant branded Twitter account for your startup, business owners should consider creating their own personal account on Twitter. Fans and followers often want to connect with the person behind the brand." – Lewis Howes, athlete, entrepreneur, and author of *The School of Greatness*

6. **Create a shareable, one-page profile flat sheet**

Find a way to show your work visually—a brochure that gives your network digestible data that supports your approach.

This is similar to the way graphic artists often use infographics to make their content consumable.

I created one of these long before they became popular with executives. I also update it regularly. I have hard copies for events I speak at, and I have a high-resolution digital version.

I have found it has created a great first impression when my network has shared it as a way to introduce me.

7. **Submit content to be published with other associations**

For example, I know that the Project Management Institute is always looking for content for papers and webinars. Maybe the association related to your craft would be interested in what you have to say.

What associations, journals, or magazines do you and your network tend to refer to? Maybe they would welcome one of your topics.

"The grass is always greener where you water it." – Unknown

8. **Volunteer to be a speaker, podcast guest, or panel member**

I have helped thousands of people by speaking at events or being a guest on a podcast. I always talk about topics I am passionate about and have experience with. That way, not only can I talk confidently about the subject, but I can also share stories of how I have experienced situations that are relevant to it.

"I always think a great speaker convinces us not by force of reasoning, but because he is visibly enjoying the beliefs he wants us to accept." – William Butler Yeats

I've spoken about Project Management, Change Management, and how to integrate them at industry conferences. I have also talked about Personal Branding and Authentic Networking. I've even taken the risk of talking about my journey from the welfare lines, foster system, and generally underprivileged beginnings to being the first in my family to attain a university degree. I went on to manage multiple departments and provided customer service to over 900K customers nationally, and became an influential leader for others before I was 30.

"A great brand is a story that's never completely told. A brand is a metaphorical story that connects with something very deep – a fundamental appreciation of mythology. Stories create the emotional context people need to locate themselves in a larger experience." – Scott Bedbury, branding consultant and CEO of Brandstrea

As a result, some of those individuals have followed up with me or continue to advocate for my content when I share it on social media platforms.

9. **Network regularly, in person**

"The richest people in the world look for and build network. Everyone else looks for work." – Robert Kiyosaki, founder of the Rich Dad Company

You need to be seen in your community as well. Plus, it's an excellent opportunity to demonstrate the small, but meaningful aspects of your personal brand. However…

"Too many individuals network with the purpose of accomplishing an immediate goal. That's not networking, that's selling." – Samuel Dergel, founder and Principal of Dergel Executive Search

I recognise that networking is not simple. To be honest, I had a lot of learning and practising to get even remotely good at networking. It can be difficult, but it is essential; therefore, I have dedicated the entire next chapter to the topic.

10. **Host your own workshops and invite target clients from your network**

If you have something you think could be helpful, introduce it to others and let them try it. In doing so, again, you are demonstrating your personal brand.

"Tell me, and I forget. Teach me, and I remember. Involve me, and I learn." – Benjamin Franklin

The thing to remember here is the same thing to remember when you write content: make sure it's coming from a place that will help your audience—from their perspective on their problems.

"A good teacher, like a good entertainer, first must hold his audience's attention, then he can teach his lesson." – John Henrik Clarke, historian and pioneering professor of African studies

Inevitably, some of the people who show up will be attracted by your solution and the solution provider—you—but won't have the time to execute your solution on their own.

So guess who they may call to make further inquiries and give you an opportunity? Yup—YOU.

11. Send links from LinkedIn and your website to your network and social circle

Entertain or help your network, when it makes sense.

Wondering about what to send?

Look at all the content you've collected or created. In the right moment, when you know a person in your network is experiencing a problem or is asking for help, send them a note with something that will help them—give them a gift. Even a simple gift of a quotation, yours or others', may make a world of difference to your network.

You'll be remembered for it.

When you are helpful and thoughtful, you will be memorable

The ways to help amplify your influence and demonstrate your authority constantly evolve. Some of the list above will stick around for a long time. Others will become untrendy, and new ways will arise. So you will need to keep an eye on the various options available to you.

The thing to remember is to provide value (from your network's perspective) in a way that aligns with your personal brand—constantly—using the approaches and tools I've provided and others you discover.

"As one person I cannot change the world, but I can change the world of one person." – Paul Shane Spear, actor and comedian.

CHAPTER 8

How to Network in Person

"Succeeding in business is all about making connections."
– Sir Richard Branson

I mentioned in Chapter 7, **How to Amplify Your Influence and Demonstrate Your Authority**, that one way to make connections is to network in person.

Networking in person is an essential skill for any consultant. It helps give you a choice of opportunities. And as you know, the more options and opportunities you have, the more often you can:

- work with your ideal clients
- do the work you love
- make the money that matches the value you deliver

"First, you have to be visible in the community. You have to get out there and connect with people. It's not called net-sitting or net-eating. It's called networking. You have to work at it." – Ivan Misner, founder and chairman of the business networking organization BNI, called the "Father of Modern Networking" by CNN and the "Networking Guru" by Entrepreneur magazine

Are you worried about bombing? Or about making a fool of yourself?

Have you ever found yourself at an event, watching the other attendees? And then you see it…it's like watching a car accident.

A group walks into the room, unsure of who should go through the door first. They are speaking over one another, interrupting. And at the same time, they are shy, looking at their phones, and not engaging with each other.

Have you been embarrassed for them? Cringed?

Then you quickly sober up and ask yourself, "Have I done that? Have others seen me be that rude? Have others laughed at me? I can't even remember how I got in the room…or who I last spoke to…" <Groan>

First, I have been that person, the one you've been embarrassed for

I was awful at networking in the past. I would struggle to know which events to attend, or I would show up and not know what to say.

No, I wasn't raised in a barn.

And yes, I was taught manners.

There have just been moments when I was so excited, or so scared of being at a networking event, that it all flew out of my head.

- I was caught at the door with others—who goes first?
- I was introduced to someone—and couldn't remember their name five minutes later.
- I wanted to make a good impression—then stumbled over what to say or how to act.

As my embarrassment climbed, I diverted my attention to my blackberry. Yes, I'm dating myself now. I got overwhelmed and felt small. I wasn't leaving the best impression, nor was I able to build my network. And as a result, my confidence floundered.

How about you?

So how did I turn it all around?

Thankfully, an incredible leader and mentor took me under her wing early in my career.

She gave me exceptional knowledge for my various career roles, but she also gave me dozens of social event opportunities.

"Find someone new to meet and help. Have ZERO agenda on how this helps you. Just make them better in some way. Seek nothing in return." – Chris Brogan, social media consultant and President of Chris Brogan Media, LLC

My mentor was a beautifully graceful and confident leader who knew how to make others in the room feel comfortable. She also taught me traditional and tasteful etiquette protocols, with a modern twist.

She not only modelled this, but she instructed me patiently and answered my endless questions about the small stuff. I learned a great deal from her because I cared to learn.

When I was with her, I felt respected: she lifted me up.

I felt I was in the presence of someone who cared, and she never once made me feel she was embarrassed to be seen with me.

"Truly great people do not feel important, they make others feel important." – Unknown

Her approach inspired me to do the same for others

It was important to me because I wanted others to know that they, too, were important.

Today, I can walk into a networking event with my head held high. I am confident and can navigate various events with perceived ease. I leave an impression on the people I meet. I stand out.

I repeatedly get feedback on how my seemingly unique approach to meeting and following up makes others feel special and comfortable. As a result, when I need to follow up, my call or email is welcomed. I am remembered, and the relationship continues to grow.

So, what's the trick?

Ever heard of the saying, "Don't Sweat the Small Stuff"? Well, I am here to proclaim—it's NOT TRUE!.

Yes, sweat the small staff—when it comes to networking in person.

"How you make others feel about themselves says a lot about you." – Boonaa Mohammed, poet and keynote speaker

Before the event

People often believe that the networking event itself is where all the effort resides. However, using the next 7 questions to prepare in advance will make networking as comfortable as possible for both you and the people you meet.

But don't worry, you're not starting from scratch. As it happens, you'll be dipping into all the great work you've done in the previous 5 chapters.

In fact, you'll find that networking is all about:

- leveraging the answers you received from your trusted advisors' feedback
- the approaches you've chosen to help amplify your personal brand
- demonstrating your authority, again and again

The only difference between networking and the work you've just finished is the filter: you'll be sharing the same information, just with a real person instead of with the internet at large.

"Luck is what happens when preparation meets opportunity." – Seneca, Roman Stoic philosopher

1. **Answer the question, what is your goal for networking?**

    Why are you networking? Is it just something you know you should do?

    Be precise about the reason you want to go to events and connect with others. Maybe you're looking for free food and drinks (that's usually a bonus). I focus on the long-term benefits. I try to be purposeful so that I don't waste my time or energy. I go to:

    - assess what's happening in my market
    - become more recognised by my peers and potential clients
    - share knowledge
    - learn about opportunities

    Whatever your reasons, determine 1 to 3 priorities before you go.

    "Networking is not collecting contacts! Networking is about planting relations." – Unknown

2. Answer the question, who do you want to meet?

Ever wonder which events would be good for you to attend? This question helps us be more targeted: to meet the people we can help or who can help us.

"There is no such thing as money problems. There are only relationship problems." – Joan Sotkin, founder and CEO of Prosperity Place

I answer these questions to narrow down which events will be valuable for me to attend:

- Who do I need to meet to achieve my goals?
- Why do I want to meet them?
- What do they tend to be interested in?
- Where do they tend to go or hang out?

3. Answer the question, why would they want to meet you?

Successful networking requires an exchange of value. You have decided who will bring value to you, now you need to bring something of value to them.

"Everybody has a problem, and if you have a solution, you can meet and help people." – Judy Robinett, entrepreneur and author of *How to Be a Power Connector: The 5-50-150 Rule*

This value could be as simple as helping someone make a new connection or sharing useful information that is easy for you to give. As I mentioned, I share my knowledge of LinkedIn and personal branding.

I decide what would be useful by asking myself these questions:

- What can I provide, easily?
- What can I help with, efficiently?
- Would anyone in my network find what I can give valuable? Why?

Over time, by asking questions and listening to the contacts I networked with, I have created several packets of information or services I am happy to share with others.

4. **Answer the question, who are you?**

Do you struggle with merely introducing yourself? I'm sure the questions you asked yourself in Chapter 5 will help, but here are a few reminders for good measure.

For a long time, I didn't know what to say besides, "Hi, I'm Tanya." There are so many facets of who I am that I didn't know where to start. So, I began by asking myself:

- What are my skills, capabilities, and strengths?
- What are my passions?

I brainstormed as many ideas as I could. Then I zeroed in on my top 3 to 5 for each question. This gave me a foundation to work from to create a decent and short phrase to introduce myself in the context of the networking event. It shifts, slightly, for each event.

"If you're always trying to be normal, you will never know how amazing you can be." – Maya Angelou

5. **Answer the question, what is your expertise?**

Are you often hired for a role and associated skills?

Maybe you are a project or program manager? An engineer? A business analyst, a strategist, or a leadership coach? These are very broad, horizontal roles.

Your role is not necessarily your *expertise*.

Expertise is expert skill, knowledge, or judgment in a specific field—this is where you have deep familiarity and experience. For example, I am often sought out as a Change Manager, which is a horizontal role.

But what gets my clients' attention is not my horizontal role, it's my:

- direct experience as an employed, budget-holding leader. I can make the difficult decisions and do the hard change projects with my teams and processes.
- ability to build or change teams and to establish performance-management systems with leaders and their teams.
- direct experience as a project manager. I run project management offices, and I know how to deliver my services within a project construct.

This is my expertise—my vertical depth. How did I clarify my expertise? I answered the following questions:

- What are my career attributes?
- What makes me stand out from my peers?
- What challenges have I faced and conquered in my career?
- What have I failed at and learned from?

I have answered these again and again. The best time to answer them is at the end of an engagement or contract when the content is fresh. If you haven't done it before, just think about your last 3 engagements and answer the questions above for each one.

"Everything that you want to be, you already are, and you're simply on the path of discovering it." – Alicia Keys, American singer-songwriter and musician

6. Answer the question, how can you be memorable?

I bet you remember particular people from networking events. Think about those you remember favourably and ask why. Why do they stand out to you?

How the other person looked at the event is likely one factor. It probably helped if they offered to help you, or if you volunteered to help them.

But the most memorable people, the ones you look forward to meeting again, always have something *more*. It's not just how they looked or that they offered to help you. The 'more' was likely that they had stories or experiences they shared with you that anchored them in your mind: they resonated with you.

You can also do this: **take inventory of your stories and experiences.**

Reflect on the experiences you've had. Then think about how they relate to:

- how you want to be known
- your expertise

- your goals
- who you want to meet

For example, I want to meet leaders who are interested in my expertise. I also look for leaders who appreciate resiliency, being a team player, and who can have fun and laugh at themselves. As a result, I share a story about how I embarrassed myself in front of an executive by falling on my ass, right in front of her desk, the first day I met her. It was a ridiculous moment! [Insert laugh track here.]

I go on to describe how, by being able to laugh together, we went on to talk about a significant change I was responsible for and that I needed this leader's help with. In the end, I won her over. We worked together for many years, persevered through what seemed like crazy and insurmountable situations, and delivered results while we cared for our teams.

To this day, we are still friends and help one another in our business endeavours.

Through sharing stories that fit the conversation and audience, I have:

- met like-minded people in my network
- made new friends

- received opportunities where my skills, approaches, and personality are appreciated

"It's hard to create what you cannot articulate. Get clear on your desires." – Jill Koenig, Goals Coach and founder of LiveYourDreams.com

Now that you've taken all that you've learned about yourself from Chapters 3 to 7 and answered the questions above, you have laid an excellent foundation for networking in person.

Now, you have a few other things to do to prepare for your next in-person networking event.

You'll find some of the following steps will sound familiar, even a bit 'old fashioned,' like the manners you may have heard your grandparents demand. However, it's practicing these small things that has helped me stand out and express the various facets of my personal brand.

"Modern-day etiquette is about behaving with grace around others, but it serves another function as well: it gives us something to fall back on in new, strange or awkward situations. Good etiquette always takes into account cultural, generational and social differences, and it allows people to handle all situations with civility and dignity." – Charles MacPherson, author of The Pocket Butler.

7. Prepare to introduce yourself or to be introduced

Practice your introduction and questions ahead of time. "My name is…, owner of… I provide…. services and products. I am currently focused on…"

8. Have your business cards ready

Hopefully, you got them designed with some available white space, on card paper that can be written on. Also, have a nice pen on you

Yes, there is still an appreciation for well-designed cards on good paper stock with room to write a note. I'll explain why this is important in the next section, During the event.

9. RSVP

See if you can learn if there will be anyone at the event you'd like to meet (whether for the first time or to follow up from a previous event). Prepare to meet them, and freshen up on any information that could help your conversation with them.

10. Arrive on time and dress appropriately

What is appropriate? It depends on the conference and related industry. You'll have to do some research to find out.

During the event

This is when the rubber hits the road, and where all your pre-work is going to come in handy. But again, there are some particular things to be aware of while you are attending the event.

"It takes 20 years to build a reputation and five minutes to ruin it. If you think about that, you'll do things differently." – Warren Buffett, chairman and CEO of Berkshire Hathaway

11. Put your phone on vibrate and put it away

If a call comes in, step away from the conversation and find somewhere private to take the call. Don't disrupt the people around you.

12. Acknowledge everyone you encounter

This includes the coat check staff, registration personnel, and waiter.

How you treat others is a direct reflection of you. And how you interact with someone who is fulfilling a 'service' role also says a lot about you.

Before I got my first professional employment, I was in the service industry. The restaurant and retail industries were how I made a living during my school years. Believe me when I say that a simple acknowledgement and thank you is always appreciated, no matter the staff's role.

It also amazed me how one customer could treat me terribly, while the next would not only acknowledge the poor treatment, but also saw all that I tried to do to be helpful.

And there is the lesson: we are all being watched, whether we are a patron, a customer, or the service staff.

Yes, there may be different cultural expectations, country to country. But still, being respectful, polite, and aware of the local customs never goes wrong.

13. Always graciously offer the door or seat at the table to the other person first

This also helps indicate you are mindful of those around you. And ladies, don't assume you get the first choice. But if you do, say thank you gracefully.

Heck, everyone, always say thank you! It never goes out of style, but it is incredible how many people don't say it, and they are remembered for it.

14. When introduced, offer to shake hands, firmly

Yes ladies, that's you too. However, also be aware of cultural differences. If the other person doesn't want to shake your hand, no problem. Follow their lead. Flexibility is necessary.

15. When meeting someone for the first time, repeat his or her name in your conversation

If you struggle with remembering names, this will help.

Personally, I am terrible with names. It's a constant effort for me to keep names top of mind. It's not that I'm not paying attention, that I don't care, or that the person left a poor impression. In fact, it's the reverse for me. I get so interested in the other person's words and story, and so caught up being curious about them, that I just don't retain their name.

I'll remember their story, what they're wearing, what's important to them, their stories about their families, how they emphasised words, and even their mannerisms—but not their name.

So, I work diligently to weave the other person's name into our conversation without sounding like a lunatic. That way, their name becomes more anchored in my memory.

16. Use the appropriate amount of formality depending on the circumstance

Mr., Mrs., Dr....

Don't know? Err on the side of being more formal, at least at first, until you are told otherwise. This is especially true outside of North America.

17. Always maintain eye contact

Don't stare, but give your entire attention to the people you meet and respond appropriately.

18. If there are more than two of you in the group, remember to 'turn the table'

Take turns engaging everyone in the group.

19. Be more interested in others, and you will be more interesting yourself

Be curious, ask questions.

"Everyone you will ever meet knows something you don't."
– Bill Nye, science educator

20. Be careful of using humour, at first

If you are meeting someone for the first time, you don't want to offend them unintentionally.

21. Lost for a conversation subject?

Say something flattering and honest about the other person; relate to them. It could be as simple as mentioning similar clothing or that you like their watch, etc.

22. Listen carefully when you meet someone

Come from a place of value. How can you help the person you just met? Ask questions like: what are you working on, what are you focused on, and how can I help you with that focus?

If you offer to help in some way (keep Chapter 7 in mind,) keep track of your commitments.

This may also be an excellent opportunity to ask for a way to contact them. If they hesitate, this is where the lovely business card and pen that you prepared before the event will come in handy. Provide your card with a clear, handwritten note of what you are willing to help them with. If they want the help, they will call or email and initiate the next level of conversation.

Your act may prompt them to offer you their information in return. If so, follow through and send them the helpful thing you mentioned.

23. Offer your business card when it's asked for

If the other person is interested in connecting after the event, they will. If not, it only cost you a bit of paper—don't worry about it afterwards.

24. Check your ego at the door

Wait until you have established credibility before you even consider challenging someone you've just met.

After the event

So, the event is done. You'll either be jazzed up by all the interesting people you met and information you learned, or, if you're an introvert like me, you may be bone tired and need to unwind and take some time to recharge.

In either case, you are not done yet. You have a few more things to cover as soon as you can. Don't take too long, as the following suggestions help you stay front of mind with those you just met.

"Social Networking that matters is helping people achieve their goals." – Seth Godin

25. Decide whom you'd like to follow up with

This is regardless of whether they gave you their contact information—this time. Create a system that works for you so you can remember the highlights of your conversation. You want to be prepared to meet them again in the future.

26. Depending on the position of the person you met, send a follow-up

This might be a LinkedIn note, a direct email, or handwritten thank-you card to recognise the value of meeting them. Note what you took away or offer to follow up on the commitment you mentioned earlier.

When you put it all together...

Preparing in advance for a networking event and being polite with excellent manners never goes out of style. When you build and live with an authentic personal brand and courteous manner, you will not only be confident at the networking event, you will help others feel comfortable, and they will remember you.

Networking used to scare the crap out of me. But with this preparation and practice, reflection and refinement, it's gotten much easier.

I still go through these questions and keep these tips in mind to improve my abilities, even after 20 years of connecting with people. And each time I do, I discover a bit more about myself, my goals, the problems that are common among the people in my network, how I can help those people, and ultimately my personal brand—in everything I do.

"Understand that networking is an ongoing process, not a discrete event. Success comes from constantly making new contacts, follow up and keeping in touch." – Unknown

Leave a positive impression that adds value, and be ready for the doors of opportunity to open.

CHAPTER 9

How to Manage Your Reputation Effectively

Guess what? We've already covered the hardest work you need to do to build your personal brand.

There's one last step: how to manage your reputation effectively

The reality is, your personal brand is 'happening' all the time—some of it is the conscious effort you put in it to build it, as we've discussed in previous chapters. Other parts of it happen unconsciously through the things you, or the people around you, do.

"Brand is no longer what we tell the consumer it is—it is what consumers tell each other it is." – Scott Cook , co-founder of Inuit

Personal branding in the digital age

Not too long ago, we could get away with just about anything. Unless someone was in a room with us at the same time, or knew us within a degree or two of separation, any faux pas or mistakes we made were soon forgotten.

Fortunately (or unfortunately,) thanks to social media, we now have countless immediate memories available and re-circulating. This is both a blessing and a curse. Today, embarrassments like misspelt Tweets, Facebook rants about crappy days with our clients, or articles shared on LinkedIn that turned out to be false can come back to haunt us.

Thankfully, you have some options for how to manage your reputation, both online and offline.

Here are a few suggestions to get you started.

What you can do in the real world

The approach I take is to check in with my clients throughout an engagement to confirm I am meeting their expectations. I don't wait until the end.

I thank them for positive feedback, and make a note if I want to add it purposefully to my personal brand.

When it comes to constructive feedback or criticism, I respond professionally and thank them. Then I determine if I want to:

- adjust and fix the cause for the feedback
- consciously include it as part of my personal brand as well—to further differentiate myself and narrow my target audience

The choice is mine.

"The keys to brand success are self-definition, transparency, authenticity and accountability." – Simon Mainwaring, author of *We First: How brands and consumers use social media to renew capitalism and build a better world*

<u>What you can do online</u>

1. **Search yourself**

    Use every possible search engine, forum, and social network that's popular in your market. Search using every possible spelling, nickname, and maiden name. You may even go so far as to search just your first name along with your known location(s).

2. **Clean up your social media accounts**

    Go through your accounts, past blogs, past comments on forums—anywhere you have frequented to make sure no 'unfortunate' posts or photos you wish never happened are still lurking.

On that note, you may do this with your friends and family too, just to be sure you won't be blindsided by someone who doesn't take your online reputation as seriously as you do. Need help? There are various services available to help you scrub the net.

3. **Update your security settings**

Make sure you've gone through all the security settings on all your online tools and adjust your privacy settings accordingly.

Review your settings regularly. These tools tend to update and change their sharing and privacy rules often and at different times of the year.

4. **Review comments posted on content that you share**

Now that you're acting on some of the items I suggested from Chapter 7, you need to be vigilant in reviewing the comments your followers leave. You need to take some risks and share your thoughts, and then take some time and listen to how people are engaging with you.

The trick here is not to take it all personally. Make sure you sift through with appropriate filters. If you're not sure, ask you trusted advisors for help.

"If they don't know you personally, don't take it personally."
– Unknown

Your reputation is determined by your clear, personal brand

All you have to do is invest in yourself and your brand and the actions you take from Chapter 7, **How to Amplify Your Influence and Demonstrate Your Authority.** This will naturally help you manage your reputation, both in the real world and online.

To finish, remember: you need to take regular action to feed your personal brand. This can mean different things to different people. I do some things quarterly and others bi-yearly or yearly. Set the pace that makes sense for the actions you will take to manage your personal brand and your reputation.

"There is no more profitable investment than investing in yourself. It is the best investment you can make; you can never go wrong with it. It is the true way to improve yourself to be the best version of you and lets you be able to best serve those around you." – Roy T. Bennett, author of *The Light in the Heart*

CHAPTER 10

What Now?

I'm confident that you now have the plan to build and manage your authentic personal brand as an independent consultant. So the question is, what's next? I would recommend you follow a few specific steps for success:

Tip 1. Take a moment to consider why you picked up this book

You picked this book up for a reason. Something sparked your interest, something spoke to you. Maybe it's because you never want to feel undervalued or taken advantage of again. Or because you want to be able to create the dream life you've always wanted. Whatever your motivation is, keep it in mind throughout your personal branding journey. That inspiration, combined with this content, will guide you in your next steps.

Tip 2. Remember my tips for implementing these tools

- Have an open mind so you can accept new ideas.
- Implement the strategies that you learn as you're reading.
- Take what works and discard what doesn't.

Apply what you learn and tweak it to make it your own. And implement bit by bit over time.

Tip 3. Make a commitment to yourself: take action

Take the first step and begin the process of revealing, building, and managing your personal brand: make a commitment to yourself to continue on this path. You may have some awkward moments. You may experience a few painful revelations. But the benefits of having a clean, authentic personal brand outweigh the small discomforts you may temporarily endure.

Tip 4. Use your free, downloadable cheat sheet

Remember the cheat sheet from Chapter 1? As a way of saying thank you for your purchase, I have provided a free cheat sheet on my website. Go to www.tanyastevenson.com/report

The cheat sheet covers the following topics to help you build your independent consulting business:

- **Goal Setting**—focus on what you need to do to create a successful business and design the life you want
- **Mindset**—shift your paradigm to help yourself take action to move your business to the next level
- **Personal Branding and Specialization**—target your ideal clients and stand out in the market
- **Marketing and Lead Generating**—set yourself up to have your choice of multiple opportunities, when *you* want them
- **Types of Contracts and Setting Terms**—position yourself and your contract for the best possible outcome
- **Negotiate**—do it with confidence

...and much, much more.

Tip 5. Check out my coaching program

After you've implemented this new content, you'll be ready for more help. I encourage you to check out my coaching program—I promise it will be the best investment you ever make in yourself. Why? It's always beneficial to have someone help guide you. But it's even better when you can learn from my mistakes, which will save you a lot more money than you will spend on my coaching program. Trust me, I know because I've already paid for them. I am more than happy to share my experiences and lessons learned if it's going to help you succeed even faster than I did. And that's the last reason: because you'll reach your goals faster.

If you're serious about improving your business as an independent consultant, this program will help you get results.

We cover in-depth information, beyond personal branding. I also provide fast-action guides and step-by-step instructions that are impossible to include in a single book. And finally, we have an opportunity to discuss aspects that are important specifically to you and your circumstances

If you're interested in my program, take a moment to book your free consultation by filling out an application form. During this free consultation, I will get to know you and your goals and will provide some suggestions for steps you can take. We'll also discuss whether this program is the right fit for you. The information you provide in the application will only be used to tailor the content to the participants. I will not pass your information along to anyone else.

>>> Go to www.tanyastevenson.com/coaching

Here's a little taste of what others have to say about the program:

"Whether you're an independent consultant just starting out or wanting to experience more success in your line of work, this is THE course for you. Tanya's expertise is evident, her energy is infectious and she keeps the content lively. The topics flow nicely and each section gives you tangible tips and tricks to action, in many cases delivering multiple benefits. I would highly recommend this program!"

- ALISON YARWOOD, LEARNING & PERFORMANCE CONSULTANT

CAN YOU DO ME A FAVOUR?

Before you go, I have one small favour to ask. Would you take 60 seconds to write a quick blurb about this book on Amazon? Reviews are the best way for independent authors (like me) to get noticed, sell more books, and spread their messages to as many people as possible.

I read every review and use the feedback to write future revisions—and even future books.

Please navigate to the book's page on Amazon in order to leave a review.

Thank you. I really appreciate your support. And thanks for checking out my book.

And finally: share your successes and frustrations with me

If you follow what I've laid out in this book, you will transform your personal, professional, and business life—I guarantee it. And I want to hear your success stories!

I hope you send me a message telling me how you are doing and how your business has changed as a result of managing your personal brand. You can reach me at tanya@standanddeliverinc.com.

Here's to your independent consulting business success!